MARVELING AT GOD'S MYSTERIES

Creative Faith

Experiences

for Youth

Tracey Marx

MARVELING AT GOD'S MYSTERIES:

Creative Faith Experiences for Youth

by Tracey Marx

Copyright © 1997 Educational Ministries, Inc.

All rights reserved. Printed in the United States of America. No portion of this book may be reproduced by any means without prior permission of the copyright owner.

ISBN 1-57438-010-9

Educational Ministries, Inc.

165 Plaza Drive

Prescott, AZ 86303

520-771-8601

Contents

An Invitation — 5

Marveling at God's Mysteries — 9

Marveling at God's Existence — 19

Marveling at God's Love — 29

Marveling at God's Power — 39

Marveling at God's Nature — 51

Marveling at God's Grace — 61

Marveling at God's Possibilities — 73

Song Resources — 81

An Invitation

Introduction

Welcome to <u>Marveling at God's Mysteries: Creative Faith Experiences for Youth</u>. This book is an invitation for you, other adult leaders and a group of youth to come together as a community to creatively experience and express your faith. Creative Faith Experiences are opportunities to speak to God and to allow God to speak to you through your imaginations. Creative Faith Experiences combine elements from worship, study and the arts, in a context that allows youth to learn, to have fun and to enjoy being together.

Creative Faith Experiences will be different for each group. Before each experience, read the chapter, choosing and adapting activities that meet the needs of your group. Ask yourselves these questions: What important events are going on in the life of the group? What important events are happening in the lives of the individuals of the group? Think about these questions as you plan each experience. Before each session, pray for your group and for their needs.

If you are leading with other adults, join with them for a time of planning and prayer before each session. Allow the other adults to lead various activities in each program. Sometimes, the transition from active to reflective activities is rather abrupt. By rotating the leadership, you will help the youth to make the transition.

I have written these sessions to take place in seven one-hour time frames, ideal for a seven-week unit in Sunday School, Youth Group, or a weekly Bible Study. However, they can be used individually, or as sessions for a weekend retreat. The time suggestions for each activity are just suggestions. Feel free to take the time that you feel the group needs, especially with the creative responses and small group sharing times.

If you have a group with mostly younger youth (ages 12-14), you may need to have an adult to facilitate each small group sharing time. Providing each participant with the questions and giving them some time to jot down their answers will help them as they come together to discuss.

This book can be used with any size group. If you have a small group of six to eight youth, stay as a group for all the sharing times. If you have a larger group, break up into manageable units and have a team of adults helping with the leadership.

Create an environment that invites marveling. Each week, youth will create things both individually and as a group. Some things will be personal and youth will want to take them home. If your space allows, hang the other creations up on bulletin boards, on the walls and doors. As the group moves through the sessions, the room will evolve as well.

Prayer is an important part of each Creative Faith Experience. Litanies involve the whole group in saying the prayer aloud. With younger groups, you may want to read the litany once through as practice, and then a second time as prayer. Poem prayers are another creative way to pray. Poem prayers are exactly that-poems that are also prayers to God. By lighting a candle before each poem prayer, you create a space that is quiet and holy. In this space, allow the words of the poem prayer to become the group's prayer to God. Encourage the youth to read the poem prayers slowly and with feeling. Each week, you will give copies of the poem prayer to each person. Encourage them to use the poem prayer during the week.

Some youth groups love to sing. Others don't. If yours is the kind of group that likes to sing, see the section at the end of the book, "Song Resources." I've listed several songs that would fit each topic, as well as songs that would be good selections to sing every week. If you don't have access to these songs, use your own selections. I haven't included singing in the suggested schedule, but feel free to make time to make a joyful noise. After the Invitation usually is a time when the youth will have energy and interest in singing. Remember how important music is to adolescents (and to all of us). Music can speak to our spirits.

Marveling at God's Mysteries is an exploration of God. This series of Creative Faith Experiences asks the questions: Who is God? How does God act in our lives and in the world? Theologically, to ask these kinds of questions is to delve into the doctrine of God. The first week, the group looks at what it means to marvel at God's mysteries. Then each week, the group explores one aspect of God: existence, love, power, nature, grace and possibilities. Although youth will be asking theological questions, Marveling at God's Mysteries is not just an intellectual quest. It is more a quest of the spirit and a quest of the imagination.

The most important thing to remember as you lead the group is that these sessions are not an attempt to solve God's mysteries, but to marvel at them. We can't know everything about God because we are human. Try to put aside desires to give pat answers to youth. Allow them to ask their questions. Share your questions. Creative Faith Experiences encourage youth to live into the questions and the answers.

May God bless the journey that you and the youth will take as you grapple with faith questions and marvel at God's mysteries!

Marveling at God's Mysteries

Session I

Preparing for the Experience:

Read Genesis 32:22-31. This is the story of Jacob's nighttime wrestling match on the banks of the River Jabbok. There are many different opinions of who Jacob's adversary is. Some say it is God. Some say it is an angel. Some say it is a man. Although youth might have questions about this, it is more important to understand that in his wrestling experience, Jacob perceived that he struggled with the divine presence. Jacob met the divine face to face, yet his life was spared. His encounter left him changed, marked by an injury to his hip and by his new name, Israel.

Gather the following: newsprint, markers, a cardboard box, a Bible, copies of the Sharing Questions, paint, paintbrushes, jars of water, copies of the litany, index cards, pencils, a hat or basket, copies of the poem prayer, a candle and matches.

Pray: God, please bless our youth group as we begin these creative faith experiences. Help us to be open to marvelling at Your mysteries. Especially be with...(fill in the needs of the members of your group). Help our group to.... Amen.

Suggested Schedule:

As Youth Arrive—15 minutes before the start of the program + 5 min.

Invitation—5 minutes

Story—5 minutes

Dramatic Encounter—5 minutes

Faith Imagining—5 minutes

Creative Response—10 minutes

Small Group Sharing—10 minutes

Litany—3 minutes

Faith Questions—7 minutes

Poem Prayer and Closing—5 minutes

As Youth Arrive:

On a chalkboard or on newsprint, write the following two headings: "A Mystery is..." and "To Marvel means..." Provide markers or chalk. As youth arrive, be available to greet them and talk to them. Encourage them to add their definitions to the two headings on the chalkboard or newsprint.

Invitation:

Welcome everyone to their first creative faith experience. Explain that today and for the next six weeks, the group is going to have an opportunity to marvel at God's mysteries. Ask for a volunteer to read the definitions of what a mystery is. Ask for another volunteer to read the definitions of what it means to marvel. Share that the word marvel means to become filled with surprise, wonder, or amazement. The word mystery means something that cannot be fully understood.

Say: "Marveling at God's mysteries means to become filled with surprise, wonder or amazed curiosity about a God we cannot completely comprehend. Our God is an awesome God! As humans we stand in awe of a God who is so much bigger than we are; so much more than we can ever understand!

"Does this mean we shouldn't try to understand? Not at all! Living out a life of faith means struggling with hard questions and trying to explain the unexplainable. But in the end to marvel at God's mysteries is to let God be God."

Story:

Tell the story "A Box of God." If you can, learn the story well enough to tell it in your own words. Walk out of the room, and walk back in carrying a cardboard box. Set the box down in the middle of the group. As you tell the story, act out the motions.

A Box of God

Once there was a man who found an empty box. "Just what I was looking for!" he said. "This will be perfect!"

He took the lid off the box. Then he took his leather, engraved Bible with gold edges and placed it in the box. He put his gold cross necklace that he always wore to church in the box too. Then he gathered his best church clothes, folded them neatly and placed them in the box. He looked in the box and nodded his head.

"Ahhh, yes!" he said. "Finally, I have a place to put God. God is here inside my box. Now God won't surprise me or confuse me. Now God won't run around interfering with my life from Monday to Saturday. I'm very interested in God on Sundays, but not the rest of the week."

The man put the lid on the box.

"Now I can put my box of God on my closet shelf, and get it out on Sundays. It will be nice and neat to carry God to church in the box.

"I had better mark my Box of God. This way, I will remember that this is the box where God lives, and not a box of garage sale items or old shoes."

(Suddenly notices that there are other people in the room.) "Oh, hello. Do you have a box to put your God in? Would you like one?"

Dramatic Encounter:

Read Genesis 32:22-31 out loud. As you read, invite someone to be Jacob and someone to be the angel. Invite them to act out the story as you read the action. Choose either two girls or two guys to be your actors.

Faith Imagining:

Invite everyone to find a comfortable position, not near anyone else. Ask them to relax and close their eyes. Ask them to let all of their worries and tensions fade away. Invite them to breathe deeply and invite the Spirit of God to be present with them, in their imaginations.

Say: "I would like to share with you a story, a story about a man who lived thousands of years ago. The man's name is Jacob. As you hear Jacob's story, I would like to invite you to become Jacob, to experience what he experienced."

(Read the following slowly, leaving pauses to allow youth to imagine the action of the story.)

> *Imagine that it is night time... You are in a dark place...outside...by the bank of a river. You hear the water rushing over the rocks... But you are not afraid. You see a figure approach you...and you acknowledge its presence. The figure doesn't frighten you...you accept it. You wonder if it is a man...an angel...could it be God?*
>
> *The strange figure comes closer to you... All of a sudden, it is fighting with you, wrestling with you... Your struggle lasts a long time, through the night...*
>
> *You hear the figure say, "Let me go, for the day is beginning." But you refuse to let go... You hold on, and continue in the struggle... Finally, you tell the figure that you will not let it go, until it blesses you... The figure asks, "What is*

your name?" You tell it your name...and it replies, "That will be your name no longer... Your new name with be "Israel" because you have struggled with God...and struggled with people...and have overcome."

Your mind starts to race. Who is this with whom you are struggling? Could it be the Lord?...

What is your struggle with God?... What is one thing that is really weighing on your mind and on your heart?... Tell God what that struggle is, right now...in the privacy of your imagination... Allow God to respond to you, to speak to you. Shhhh, listen...

You leave the place of your struggle...knowing that because you have seen God face to face, you are changed. You are a new person... The sun rises before you and morning comes. You are ready for your new life... When you are ready, open your eyes and come back to this space.

Small Group Sharing:

Divide youth into groups of three or four. Provide a copy of the Sharing Questions for each group. Ask each group to choose a leader to report back to the larger group.

Sharing Questions

1. How easy was it for you to imagine this scene of struggle?

2. What did it feel like to wrestle with the figure? Did you feel like you were losing or winning?

3. Did you feel frightened, excited, nervous?

4. Did you feel changed, different after your experience of struggle?

5. What are some struggles you have with God?

After five minutes or so, have the small groups join together. Ask the leaders from each small group to share their answers to questions 2, 3 and 4.

Creative Response:

Give each person a sheet of newsprint, and provide paint, paintbrushes and jars of water. Invite them to paint an image or a feeling from their imagination experience. Suggest that they don't think too hard about what to paint, rather painting whatever they feel at the moment.

When they are finished, spread out the paintings in a line. As a group, walk down the length of the line, stopping at each person's creation for a moment.

Litany:

Pass out copies of this litany, and ask one of the youth to be the leader.

A Litany of God's Mysteries

One: God, we marvel at the mystery of You

All: And Your presence with us.

One: At school, at home, at work, at church,

All: With friends, with family, with our group.

One: Help us, God, to never put you in a box,

All: To never think we have You all figured out.

One: Help us to be open to all the ways

All: That You touch our lives and hearts and minds.

One: Help us with our problems and struggles

All: And all the things that worry us each day.

One: Be with us and bless us by Your touch,

All: Leaving us forever changed. Amen.

Faith Questions:

Form a circle. Pass out index cards and pencils. Ask youth to think about one question that they have about God, something that has always seemed to be a mystery to them.

Place a hat or a basket in the middle of the circle. Invite them, when they are finished writing their question, to place their cards in the basket. When everyone has finished, mix up the cards in the hat or basket, and then give a card to each person.

Say: "We all have faith questions and struggles. Even adults. Even ministers. This is normal. And we don't always receive answers to our faith questions. But even though we don't always receive answers, it's still important to ask the questions and to struggle with the answers."

Go around the circle and have everyone read the question that is on their card. After each person is finished, have them put the card back into the basket or hat, and have the whole group respond, "We marvel at Your mysteries, O God."

Create a Closing:

Explain that as a group, you will now have an opportunity to create a closing that you will use to end your time together for this experience and for the next six weeks. Some suggested closings are:

1. **The Pulse:** Standing in a circle, pass a "pulse" around the group by squeezing hands.

2. **The Group Hug:** The group stands in a circle with arms around each other's shoulders. On the count of three, the group steps in toward the center, creating a giant hug.

Allow the group to create a closing that is meaningful to them. When they have decided on their closing, explain that you will end each of your times together with a poem prayer (which is a prayer to God written in the form of a poem) and then the group's closing.

Poem Prayer:

Gather in a circle and place a candle in the center of the circle. Ask for a volunteer to light the candle. If you can, turn off some lights in the room. Pass out copies of the poem prayer and ask for two volunteers to read the poem prayer in turn, slowly and with feeling.

*As Jacob wrestled with You, O God,
so also let us wrestle
with the questions that our faith asks.
Help us to ask hard questions.
Help us to resist easy answers.
Help us in our struggle to figure out who You are,
who You can be for us,
and who we are in response to You.
And most of all, eternal God
help us to marvel at the mystery
of not always having everything figured out.
Loving God, do not let go of us,
but hold on, and bless us by Your touch,
leaving us forever changed.
Give to us a new vision, for our lives and our world,
praising You now, until we see You face to face.
Amen.*

Closing:

Say: "In our time together, we have marveled at the mysteries of God. This week, as you listen to music, read books and watch T.V. or movies, pay attention to the questions that the characters are asking. Are any of their questions faith questions? That is, do any of their questions marvel at God's mysteries?"

End with the group's chosen closing.

Marveling at God's Existence

Session 2

Preparing for the Experience:

Read Psalms 8, 19, 24, 29, 66, 84, 89, 96, & 104. The word "psalm" comes from the Greek word "psalmos", which was used by translators for the Hebrew word "mizmor" or song. The book of Psalms is a collection of 150 songs, prayers and other compositions. Psalter is another word that is used to identify this book. The word psalter comes from the Greek word, "psalterion," which is a stringed instrument. Some scholars believe that the psalms were written for worship in ancient Israel, especially at the Jerusalem Temple. The psalms that are used in this experience are psalms of praise and celebration. They celebrate God's existence in the world. When we marvel at the existence of God or question the existence of God, often our words turn into art, that is, into poetry or psalms.

Youth need a safe space to reveal their theological questions. They need to know they are not the only ones who have doubts or confusions about God's existence.

Gather the following: Psalm quotes, small squares of construction paper, basket or hat, markers, copies of the litany, Bibles (one for every two participants), copies of the Sharing Questions, pencils, copies of "Create Your Own Psalm," copies of the poem prayer, a candle and matches.

Pray for your time together: Holy One, we marvel at the mystery of Your presence with us. Help us as we spend time together as a group, pondering the perplexity of Your existence in our lives. Help us to create a spirit of openness in which the youth will feel free to ask questions and to express beliefs and disbeliefs. Help our group to... Be especially with... Amen.

Suggested Schedule:

As Youth Arrive—15 minutes before the start of program + 5 minutes

Invitation & Skits—25 minutes

Litany—3 minutes

Question and Answer Psalms—5 minutes

Small Group Sharing—10 minutes

Psalm Creations—7 minutes

Poem Prayer and Closing—5 minutes

As Youth Arrive:

Before the event starts, write the following quotes on large pieces of construction paper. Use different colors of paper.

"O Lord, our Sovereign, how majestic is your name in all the earth! You have set your glory above the heavens!"

Psalm 8:1 on **blue** paper

"The heavens are telling the glory of God; and the firmament proclaims his handiwork."

Psalm 19:1 on **green** paper

"The earth is the Lord's and all that is in it, the world, and those who live in it."

Psalm 24:1 on **red** paper

"Ascribe to the Lord, O heavenly beings, ascribe to the Lord glory and strength."

Psalm 29:1 on **yellow** paper

"Make a joyful noise to God, all the earth!"

Psalm 66:1 on **orange** paper

"How lovely is your dwelling place, O Lord of hosts!"

Psalm 84:1 on **pink** paper

"I will sing of your steadfast love, O Lord, forever."

Psalm 89:1 on **purple** paper

"O sing to the Lord a new song; sing to the Lord, all the earth."

Psalm 96:1 on **white** paper

"Bless the Lord, O my soul. O Lord my god, you are very great."

Psalm 104:1 on **gray** paper

Hang the quotes from the ceiling or on the walls. Cut out 4" squares of construction paper, using the same colors as you used for the quotes. Cut enough squares so that there is one square for each person in the group. Put the squares in a basket or hat.

As the youth arrive, greet them and be available to talk with them. Have each youth pull a construction paper square out of the hat or basket. Provide markers and have them write on the paper, "Is there a God?" Tell them to keep this to use in a later activity.

Invitation:

Welcome youth to another Creative Faith Experience. Say: "Today, we marvel at the mystery of God's existence. Does God exist and how can we know that God exists? We're going to spend some time thinking and wondering about God's existence and marvel at one of faith's greatest mysteries."

Skits:

Divide into small groups of four or five. Tell each group that they have 10-15 minutes to come up with a skit, entitled IS THERE A GOD? Tell them it can be modern day or historic. It can be any setting, any number of characters, etc. It can be funny or serious.

By letting them create their own skits, they will bring to the experience their own questions and their own thoughts about the subject of God's existence.

However, if they get stuck or if the group are mostly younger youth, (ages 12-14) you might want to give each group one of these skit starters.

SKIT STARTERS

1. Two sisters are watching television. One says to the other, "I don't believe in God. Do you?"

2. Some members of a youth group are doing a community service project in a park and a boy from their school comes along. "You don't believe in this God stuff, do you?"

3. A friend's mother dies. You are at the funeral, sitting next to your friend. The minister gets up to talk. Your friend looks at you and says, "I'm never going to believe in God again."

4. Some girls at a slumber party are playing Truth or Dare. One of the girls is asked, "Do you believe in God?" She answers "I don't know if I believe in God. What do the rest of you think?"

5. In Science class, you are learning about evolution. A girl raises her hand and asks the teacher, "Do you believe in God?"

After 10-15 minutes or so, come together as a larger group and share skits.

Litany:

Pass out copies of the litany. Ask one of the youth to be the leader.

Litany of God's Existence

One: God we marvel at the mystery

All: That You are God.

One: Sometimes we ask ourselves

All: Is there a God?

One: Help us in our doubting,

All: In our questioning and struggling,

One: To be reminded of You

All: And Your presence with us.

One: Be with us God,

All: Remind us and love us

One: In Jesus' name,

All: Amen.

Question and Answer Psalm:

Say: "The book of Psalms is an amazing collection of songs and poetry. Reading through the words, it is easy to see how the writers really struggled with their faith and how they marveled at God's mysteries."

Ask each person to find a partner, who has the same color of construction paper square. Once they have found partners, have them choose one person to be the "psalmist" and one person to be the "questioner."

Give each set of partners a Bible, and have them find the psalm that matches their construction paper color. Explain that they will read the entire psalm out loud, having the "psalmist" read one verse and the "questioner" respond, "Is there a God?"

Small Group Sharing:

Have two partners join another group of two. Provide a copy of the Sharing Questions for each group. Encourage them to think about these questions, and to share honestly. Ask each group to choose a leader to report back to the larger group.

Sharing Questions

1. Have you ever had a time when you weren't sure that God existed?
2. When did you first believe in God?
3. Do you know anyone who doesn't believe in God?
4. What helps you to know that God exists?
5. Do you think it is good to ask the question, Is there a God?

When five minutes have passed, have the group join together. Ask for the representatives from each small group to share their answers to questions 4 and 5.

Psalm Creations:

Hand out paper and pencils and copies of "Create Your Own Psalm." Explain that they will now have an opportunity to write their own psalms. Encourage the youth not to worry about spelling or grammar, but to write the first thing that comes to mind.

Create Your Own Psalm

Line 1—Address and Praise God

_____

Line 2—Describe a place where you sense God's existence the most

_____

Line 3—Tell something God has done for you

_____

Line 4—Rewrite line 3 in different words

_____

Line 5—Tell God about a struggle you have

_____

Line 6—Ask God to be with you in your struggle

_____

Line 7—Repeat Line 1

_____

Line 8—Repeat Line 2

_____

Ask if anyone would like to share his/her psalm.

Poem Prayer:

Gather in a circle with a candle at the center. Ask for a volunteer to light the candle. Turn off some lights in the room. Pass out copies of the poem prayer and ask for three volunteers to read the poem prayer in turn.

*Are you there
God?
I wonder.
Are you there, God,
Even when I wonder?
Even when I doubt?
Whisper to me in the
stillness and the darkness
of the night
when I am alone,
and feeling overwhelmed
Remind me that You
are there!
Amen.*

Closing:

Say: "Today, we have marveled at the mystery of God's existence. We have explored the psalms and how the psalmists sensed God. This week, try to take some time to talk to your parents or other adults. Ask them if they have ever had doubts about God's existence. Ask them how they know that God exists."

End with the group's closing.

Marveling at God's Love

Session 3

Preparing for the Experience:

Read the Scriptural promises about God's love for us: John 16:27; 1 John 4:7-12; Jeremiah 31:3; Zephaniah 3:17; John 3:16; 1 John 4:16; 2 Thessalonians 2:16-17.

If there is one clear message that we receive repeatedly from Scripture, it is that God loves us and cares about us. The writers of the Bible searched for metaphors to describe God's love: God is like a shepherd loving his sheep (Psalm 23), like a mother rocking a new born babe in her arms (Isaiah 66:13), like a father who responds to the cries of his children. (Romans 8:15-16).

God is love. This is a central tenet of the doctrine of God. A seminary professor once said that the phrase "God is love" is the lens through which the rest of Scripture and all Christian doctrine and should be judged.

Teenagers need to know that they are loved. Many feel profoundly unloved by family and peers. Help them to explore the mystery of God's love and to feel the power of how God's love can impact their lives.

Gather the following: 8-foot piece of paper from large roll, markers, pencils, construction paper, scissors, tape, balloons with Scripture Promises inside, Bibles, Sharing Bags with Sharing Questions inside, copies of the litany, red construction paper hearts, glue, copies of the poem prayer, a candle and matches.

Pray for your time together: God of love, surround our youth group with Your presence during our time together. Shower us with Your love and with Your acceptance. Amen.

Suggested Schedule:

As Youth Arrive—15 minutes before start of program + 10 minutes

Invitation—5 minutes

Faith Imagining—10 minutes

Balloon Pop Promises—7 minutes

Small Group Sharing—10 minutes

Litany—3 minutes

Valentines from God—5 minutes

Story—5 minutes

Poem Prayer and Closing—5 minutes

As Youth Arrive:

Create a banner by cutting a large 8-foot piece of paper from a large roll and lay it on a table. On the banner, in large letters, write the words, "We know that God loves the world because...." Provide markers.

As youth arrive, greet them and ask them to add something to the banner that finishes this sentence. They can write something in words, or draw a picture.

Also, provide pencils, construction paper and scissors and ask them to make two footprints by tracing their feet on construction paper, and cutting them out. They can set their footprints aside, to be used in a later activity.

Invitation:

Hang up the banner on a wall, and gather the group around it. Welcome the group to another Creative Faith Experience. Explain that today you will be marveling at the mystery of God's love for each one of us.

Have the group look at the banner. Invite each person to share what they have created by saying, "We know that God loves the world because..." and then explaining what they have written or drawn.

Faith Imagining:

Invite everyone to get into a comfortable position, not too close to anyone else, and to close their eyes. Suggest that they begin to relax, and to let worries and concerns of their day slip from their minds. Ask that they concentrate on their breathing, breathing out worries and concerns, and breathing in deeply.

Read the following slowly, allowing pauses, then continuing when you sense group participants are ready.

Allow your imagination to take you to a peaceful place. You can create this place to be whatever you want. It might be a mountaintop. It might be on the beach next to the ocean. It might be in your room. There is no one else there at this place. Take a few moments to imagine yourself in this peaceful place.

As you look around you, you begin to think about all of the people who love you. You think of them one by one. As you name a person in your mind, his/her face comes to you very clearly, almost as if that person were right there with you. Each face stays with you as you think of another. You might see your mother...your father...your sisters....your brothers....grandparents...other family members...your best friends...other friends...other adults, maybe coaches or teachers or your minister or youth group leaders. You are surrounded by faces of people who love you, who care about you...

You allow yourself to feel loved, incredibly loved. You feel the love around you. You can almost feel the warmth of this love... You can almost see the light of this love... You breathe in deeply and the love fills your body, your spirit, your mind.

The faces that surround you begin to fade, but the warmth and the light do not fade. Soon you are alone once more, but you do not feel alone. You feel a presence of love all around you. You hear a voice within your imagination speak to you. My precious, precious child, I love you and will never, ever leave you...

You know in your imagination that the one who spoke to you, the one who loves you is God... You think about the words you heard, I love you and will never, ever leave you... You breathe in deeply, feeling loved. You breathe out slowly, feeling loved and cared for.

You stay a few more moments in this place of your imagination... When you are ready, open your eyes.

Balloon Pop Promises:

Before the session, cut enough slips of paper so that there is one for every participant. On each slip, write down the Scripture reference to one of the Bible Promises of Love. Put each one in an uninflated balloon. Blow up the balloons and tie them. (You will want to have some help to do this, or a handy balloon pump, an inexpensive cardboard tube contraption found in novelty stores.) Have the balloons available, perhaps in a large trash bag.

Say that from the time we are very young, we learn a song that God loves us, that Jesus loves us, and that we know this because our Bible "tells us so." Ask for a volunteer to say the words to the song, "Jesus Love Me."

*Jesus loves me, this I know
For the Bible tells me so.
Little ones to him belong.
They are weak, but he is strong.*

Have youth stand up and gather in a circle. Scatter the balloons inside the circle and tell them that on your word, they are to pop one (and only one!) of the balloons as fast as they can. Tell them that the balloons contain a promise from God.

When everyone has popped their balloon, provide Bibles and have them look up their Scripture reference. Have each youth read their promise aloud.

Promises of Love

1. John 16:27

2. 1 John 4:7-12

3. Jeremiah 31:3

4. Zephaniah 3:17

5. John 3:16

6. I John 4:16

7. 2 Thessalonians 2:16-17

Small Group Sharing-Sharing Bags

Ahead of time, create Sharing Bags out of brown lunch bags. Copy the Sharing Bag Questions so that you have one sheet of questions and one bag for each small group that you will have. Cut the questions into slips of paper and fold them two or three times. Then place them in the bag. Each sharing bag should have all 15 questions.

Break into small groups of four or five. Pass out sharing bags, with these questions on slips of paper in each bag. Explain that each person should pull a slip out the bag and either answer the question or complete the sentence. Encourage them to share as much or as little as they feel comfortable with. (Note: The questions are written so that youth can answer either with statements about youth in general or they could answer more personally about themselves.)

Sharing Bag Questions

1. Do you think most teens feel loved by the mother? Why or why not?

2. Do you think most teenagers feel loved by their father? Why or why not?

3. Do you think most teenagers feel love from their step-parents? Why or why not?

4. Do you think that most teenagers feel love from their brothers or sisters? Why or why not?

5. It's hard to know that God loves you because...

6. Love is sometimes hard to talk about because...

7. God definitely loves the world because...

8. If I were God, I would have a hard time loving some people because...

9. If I were a parent, I would have a hard time loving my teenager when he or she...

10. Do you think loving someone means that you love everything that person does?

11. Can God love you and still want you to change some things in your life?

12. Does God love everyone or just some people?

13. Does God love some more than others, or does God love everyone equally?

14. The easiest way to explain God's love for us is to say that...

15. It's hard to always remember that God loves us because...

Litany:

Pass out copies of the litany. Ask one of the youth to be the leader.

A Litany of God's Love

One: God of love, we give You thanks!

All: God of love, we give You praise!

One: For the times that You love us,

All: Even when we don't feel lovable.

One: For the times when You care about us,

All: Even when we think no one cares.

One: For the times when You are interested in what we have to say,

All: Even when we aren't sure what to say.

One: Lord, we are quick to receive Your promises.

All: Help us to be just as quick to believe them.

One: We love You, and we thank You for Your love.

All: We pray in the name of Jesus, who taught us how to love You, and who taught us how to love each other. Amen.

Valentines from God:

Pass out red hearts cut from construction paper. Provide markers and glue. Invite youth to create a valentine from God to themselves, telling them how much God loves them. Encourage them to write or to draw on their valentine, and to glue their Scripture Promise to the heart.

Story:

Tell the story, "Footprints." As you tell it, invite youth to help you, by acting out various parts. If your room environment permits, after the story is told, have youth tape their footprints to the wall in the same pattern that they are on the ground (two sets going to one set). This will be a reminder of the story over the next weeks.

Footprints

(adapted story of Margaret Fishback Powers)

One night, a man had a dream. *(Invite a youth to lie down, as asleep).* He dreamed he was walking along the beach with the Lord. Across the sky flashed scenes from his life. For each scene, he noticed two sets of footprints in the sand: one belonging to him, and the other to the Lord. *(Invite half of the youth to set their footprints down, so their are two sets of footprints making a journey.)*

When the last scene of his life flashed before him, he looked back at the footprints in the sand. He noticed that many times along the path of his life there was only one set of footprints. He also noticed that it happened at the very lowest and saddest times in his life. *(Have the other half of the youth create a path with only one set of footprints.)*

This really bothered him and he questioned the Lord about it. "Lord, you said that once I decided to follow you, you'd walk with me all the way. But I have noticed that during the most troublesome times in my life, there is only one set of footprints. I don't understand why when I needed you most you would leave me."

The Lord replied, "My precious child. I love you and would never leave you. During your times of trial and suffering, when you see only one set of footprints, it was then that I carried you."

Poem Prayer:

Form a circle and place a candle in the middle. Ask for volunteers to light the candle and turn off the lights. Pass out copies of the poem prayer and ask for two volunteers to read the poem prayer in turn.

*Holy One,
You are love
Filling the empty spaces and places
In our hearts and spirits.
You are love
Holding our trembling hands,
Healing the brokenness inside.
You are love
Wiping away our tears and our fears,
Embracing us and holding us near.
You are love
You are love,
That holds on to us,
And never lets us go.
Amen.*

Say: "Today, we have spent time together marveling at the mystery of God's love. As you leave this place and go home, to school and all the places that you live your life, remember that God loves you, that God cares about you, and that you are never alone. If there is a time this week that you feel lonely (and we all do at times) remember this experience we've had together. Remember that God never leaves you alone."

End with your group's closing.

Marveling at God's Power

Session 4

Preparing for the Experience:

Read Exodus chapters 3-14. The story of the Exodus is one of the central stories of the Jewish faith. The Exodus out of Egypt is a paradigmatic story. That is, the theme of God saving the chosen people, calling them from bondage, down into the water and up into freedom becomes a paradigm or structure that other theological stories are built around. In the Christian tradition, baptism reminds us of the Exodus. There is no story from the Hebrew Scriptures that is more important to understand.

It was not until many centuries after the birth of Christ that people had access to the written word. Before that, stories were communicated orally. The power of a story, when communicated by a gifted storyteller, is that it invites its listeners to participate in the action of the story, to experience its highs and lows, to assume a role and vicariously experience what the characters experiences.

In this Creative Faith Experience, the group will tell the story of the Exodus to each other as a way to enter into the mystery of God's power.

Gather the following: newspaper clippings, newsprint or posterboard, cards with the sentences on them, a puppet or marionette, a clock, copies of the Sharing Questions, copies of "Telling the Exodus Story," pencils, Bibles, copies of the litany, index cards, copies of the poem prayer, a candle and matches.

Pray for your time together: God of power and majesty, we praise You for who You are and who You can be in our lives. Prepare each of our hearts and minds as we come together to marvel at the mystery of Your power. Be with each of the youth, in their questioning and in their faith journey. Help our group to... Be especially with... Amen.

Suggested Schedule:

As Youth Arrive—15 minutes before start of program + 5 minutes

Invitation—2 minutes

Small Group Sharing—10 minutes

The Exodus

   Preparing—7 minutes

   Telling the Story—15 minutes

Litany—3 minutes

Story—3 minutes

Creative Response—5 minutes

Secret Sculpture—5 minutes

Poem Prayer and Closing—5 minutes

As Youth Arrive:

Gather newspaper clippings that speak of tragic events or sad news. Put the newspaper clippings out on a table, so that youth can look at them as they arrive. On newsprint or posterboard, have the following sentence printed, "What kind of power does God have?"

As each person arrives, greet them and encourage them to look at the various articles and to think about the question.

Invitation:

Ahead of time, write sentences on the cards. Also, have a clock and a puppet or marionette available.

Pass out index cards, each with one of the following sentences on them. Have the youth read the sentences out loud.

- A child dies.
- A young woman is paralyzed in a diving accident.
- A sports team loses.

- A man is laid off from his job.
- A baby is born with several disabilities.
- A tornado kills 15 and destroys the homes of 50.
- A race of people is enslaved for hundreds of years.
- Millions of people are systematically tortured and killed.

Say, "From disappointments to tragedies to terrible suffering, we ask faith questions: Who is responsible for this? Who is in control? Where in the world is God?

"Today we are going to marvel at the mystery of God's power. We will ask these questions:

"What kind of power does God have?

"How does God act in the world?

(Hold up the puppet.) "Is God the puppet master, pulling our strings, telling us where to move and how to walk each step we take?

(Hold up the clock.) "Or is God more like a clock maker, having made the world, God sits back and watches it tick, not involving God's self in the world's affairs or problems?

"Or is the answer somewhere in-between, is God intimately involved in human history, and especially in our sufferings, but not controlling our every move?

"What God does in the world and the way God interacts with our lives lifts up the mystery of God's power. This is one of the most important mysteries of faith to which there are no easy answers."

Small Group Sharing:

Divide into groups of three or four, with each group taking one of the newspaper articles. Ask each group to read the article out loud, and to think about these questions. Have each group choose a leader, who will report back to the large group.

Sharing Questions

1. What happened in this news story? What is going on?

2. How do you think God was involved in this event, if at all?

3. Did God cause this event to happen?

4. Could God have prevented this event from happening?

5. Does God give humans the freedom for this kind of thing to happen?

6. Do you think anything positive came out of this event? If so, was God involved in this positive aspect?

Gather back in the large group. Ask the leader from each small group to share their answers to questions 1, 2 and 6. After each small group shares, have them tape or glue their article to the poster with this phrase written on it, "What kind of power does God have?"

The Exodus:

Give each youth a portion of the story of the Exodus. If you have more than 17 youth, have them work in partners. If you have less than 17, give some parts to other adult leaders or take several sections for yourself.

1.	Chapter 3	The burning bush
2.	Chapter 4:1-9	God gives signs to Moses
3.	Chapter 4:10-31	God chooses Aaron to help Moses
4.	Chapter 5	Moses speaks to Pharaoh
		Pharaoh says they must gather straw
		The Israelites complain
5.	Chapter 6:1-13, 26-30	Moses speaks to God
6.	Chapter 7:1-13	Aaron's staff becomes a snake
7.	Chapter 7:14-25	The first plague—water turned to blood
8.	Chapter 8:1-15	The second plague—frogs
9.	Chapter 8:16-19	The third plague—gnats
10.	Chapter 8:20-32	The fourth plague—flies
11.	Chapter 9:1-7	The fifth plague—disease
12.	Chapter 9:8-12	The sixth plague—boils
13.	Chapter 9:13-35	The seventh plague—thunder and hail
14.	Chapter 10:1-20	The eighth plague—locusts
15.	Chapter 10:21-29	The ninth plague—darkness
16.	Chapter 11:1-10	The tenth plague—death of the first-born
17.	Chapter 12:21-32	Leaving Egypt

Make enough copies of "Telling the Exodus Story" so that every person has one. Give youth time to read their portion of the story and to learn it well enough to tell it to the rest of the group.

Telling The Exodus Story

1. Your part of the Exodus story_____

2. Become familiar with your part. Find a quiet space and read your part of the story to yourself. In the space below, write down some key words that remind you of the events that happen in your portion of the story.

3. Practice telling the story in your own words. Telling the story brings it to life, much more so than reading it out loud. Be ready to help tell the story by sharing what has happened in your part. Try to be creative by using different voices for different characters and by using an energetic storytelling voice. Practice telling your story without reading directly from the Bible.

Telling the Exodus Story:

Gather as a group and introduce the story. Say: "Besides the cross and the resurrection, there is no story more important to our experience as God's people. This story has been told countless times, in many places and languages, in many settings just like the one you are in right now.

"Hear the beginning of the story of the Exodus of the Israelites out of Egypt. Listen especially for how God is with God's people. God is in the midst of their struggling. In the midst of the sufferings."

Have each youth or group of youth tell their portion of the story in turn.

Litany:

Pass out copies of this litany, and ask one of the youth to be the leader.

A Litany of God's Power

One: As You revealed Yourself to Moses at the burning bush,

All: Reveal Yourself to us, O Lord, in this time and space.

One: Call us to what You want us to do in this world,

All: And remind us that You will be with us, helping us to speak.

One: Empower and strengthen us to work for justice,

All: And to end suffering and all forms of slavery.

One: Help us to stand up against the Pharaohs of our day,

All: And to speak for You and in Your name.

One: Help us not to seek signs and wonders,

All: But to seek the power in Your words and in Your promises.

One: Remind us that You will never let Your people go,

All: As we journey toward the promised land of life with You.

Story:

Tell the story "And" by Janet Wolf, a United Methodist pastor in Nashville, Tennessee. (Videotaped for the *Questions of Faith V Series*, produced by UMCom Productions, and distributed by Ecufilm. Used with the author's permission.)

And?

When I was growing up, I would come home from school, and go tell my grandmama the stories of the day. She was the one who had time for the details. She would listen as I poured out my heart and explained why my sister might have gotten better grades but I really worked harder. How unfair life was. How rotten it was to always be the last one chosen for a sport even though I was truly good and nobody had yet recognized this talent I had.

And my grandmama used to listen with great patience to all these stories. But she would always ask me the same question at the end. The question was, "And?" There was only one right answer to this question. The answer was, "I'm going on anyhow."

No matter how many times I argued with her, the question was always the same and there was no other acceptable answer.

I'd say, "If I knew where I was going, I'd answer you. If I knew how I was going to get there. I would say that if I thought I was going anywhere. But you know I'm not really sure about this whole thing."

She would sit, she would listen and then she'd say, "And?" And you couldn't leave the room until you said it. You could sit in silence. You could be stubborn. But you weren't leaving the room until you said, "I'm going on any-

how."

It was for her a rock bottom faith statement. It meant no matter what, God is in the midst of this and so you can and you will and you must go.

Years later, I was sitting by her bed. She was dying and she said to me, "I need to hear you say it again, so I'm going to ask. And?"

I couldn't get anything out.

"And?"

I couldn't get anything out.

She said, "I know that you hear me and I know you know death is coming and I want you to answer. And?"

Finally I said, "I'm going on anyhow."

She said, "Yes you are, child! And I just want you to know that God's going to be asking you that question each and every day of your life. And I will be able to hear your answer. It better be loud and it better be clear. Every time God says, "And?" you say, "I'm going on anyhow."

Creative Response:

Pass out index cards. Have youth write the word "And" on one side of the card. Then invite them to find a comfortable position and to relax.

Say: "Think about a time when something very sad or overwhelming happened in your life. It could be something that happened recently or a long time ago. *(Pause for a minute or two.)* Try to remember how you felt when this event happened. How did you feel toward God at the time? Did you sense that God was with you? Did you feel that God had let you down? In looking back, can you think of anything good that happened in the midst of this sad or even terrible time? Imagine that God is with you, asking you the question, "And?" How do you respond? Can you respond, "I'm going on anyhow." Or do you have a different response? When you are ready, open your eyes, and write a response to God on the back of the card."

Secret Sculpture:

Explain to the group that they will now have an opportunity to become a sculpture. Choose one person to be the sculptor. The rest of the group will be the "clay." The "clay" needs to stand in an open area and be completely still and quiet. The sculptor moves the hands, arms, heads and legs of the "clay" to create the sculpture. The "clay" does not move on its own, but cooperates in what movement the sculptor wants. Neither the "clay" nor the sculptor talks.

Show the sculptor the following Secret Sculpture message about what she or he is to sculpt, but don't let the rest of group know. The task of the rest of the group is to guess what the secret sculpture is.

Secret Sculpture Message

When Pharaoh told Moses and Aaron to take the Israelites out of Egypt, it was in the middle of the night. The Israelites (men, women and children) took all their herds and flocks of animals with them. They also took bread in bowls that had not finished rising. They wrapped the bowls in their cloaks and carried them on their shoulders.

Your task as the sculptor is to create this scene of the Israelite's confusing, night departure from Egypt.

When the sculptor is done, have the "clay" try to guess what they have become. As a clue tell them the scene is taken from a certain point in the Exodus story.

Poem Prayer:

Gather together in a circle. Put a candle in the center of the circle and have one of the youth light it. Turn down the lights. Ask for two volunteers to read the poem prayer. Encourage them to read slowly and with feeling.

> *O God, we marvel at the mystery*
> *of Your power in our lives,*
> *in Your role in our stories.*
> *As You held onto Moses,*
> *hold on to each of us, God*
> *and be with us as we journey*
> *through dangers and foreign lands.*
> *Help us to name our oppressors—*
> *those things that hold on to us and keep us down.*
> *Free us from those things that keep us from*
> *entering Your promised land and Your promised life.*
> *Amen.*

Closing:

Say: "Today, we have marveled at the mystery of God's power. We have entered into the Exodus story and have traveled with the Israelites out of Egypt and into their search for the promised land. This week, try to watch the news or read the front page of the newspaper. Ask yourself how God might be involved in some of the events going on in the world." End with the group's closing.

Marveling at God's Nature

Session 5

Preparing for the Experience:

Read Acts chapter 1-2. This is the story of Pentecost. Pentecost is called the birthday of the church, when the gift of the Holy Spirit was given by God to Christians who were wondering what to do now that Jesus had died and gone to be with God.

The Spirit of God had of course, been present through the Hebrew Scripture. But the story of Pentecost was a way of clearly stating that the Spirit would be the aspect of God that would comfort and encourage new Christians as they were trying to make sense of the death of their leader.

The story of Pentecost is a good one for thinking about the mystery of God's nature because all three aspects of God take a role in this story: God the Creator, Jesus Christ and the Holy Spirit. The Trinity is probably the most baffling of God's mysteries. How can God be three, yet one?

As youth contemplate the mystery of the Trinity, they will begin to integrate many things that they have learned about the three "persons" of God into one marvelous mystery.

Gather the following: dot stickers (3 different colors), construction paper, scissors, markers, Trinity cards, Trinity phrases written down on newsprint or posterboard, tape, copies of Dramatic Encounter, fans, streamers (red, yellow and orange), copies of the litany, copies of the Sharing Questions, drawing paper and pastels, index cards and pencils, copies of the poem prayer, a candle and matches.

Pray for your time together: God of all creation, Creator, Redeemer and Sustainer, be with us as we gather to marvel at the mystery of your nature. Be with each youth in their questioning and in their search for answers. Help our group to... Be especially with... Amen.

Suggested Schedule:

As Youth Arrive—15 minutes before start of program + 5 minutes

Invitation—2 minutes

Understanding the Trinity—5 minutes

Dramatic Encounter—10 minutes

Litany—3 minutes

Creative Movement—5 minutes

Small Group Sharing—10 minutes

Creative Response—10 minutes

Trinity Prayers—5 minutes

Group Poem Prayer and Closing—5 minutes

As Youth Arrive:

Have dot stickers of three colors. As youth arrive, greet them, give them each a dot, and ask them to put it somewhere on their body, so that it is visible.

Put pieces of construction paper, scissors and markers on a table. Ask youth to cut a large triangle out of a piece of construction paper. In the three corners of the triangle, they should draw three different things they like to do, or three different roles that they play in their lives. (For this activity, you might want to have your own triangle finished as an example.)

Invitation:

Say: "Today, we are going to marvel at the mystery of God's Nature. Usually we think of God in three ways. We think of God as the Creator. We think of Jesus Christ, who was God in human form. And we think of the Holy Spirit. Does anyone know the name that we usually use for these three ways of thinking about God?" (Allow time for answers.)

"The Trinity is another way of describing the three roles that God takes. Each of us takes different roles in our lives, even though we are only one person."

Have each person share what is on their triangle.

Understanding the Trinity:

Ask the youth to get in three groups, according the color of their dot.

Before the event, create 30 Trinity cards. Write "God" on ten cards, "Jesus Christ" on ten cards and "The Holy Spirit" on the ten cards. Give each of the three groups a set of ten cards.

On a newsprint or posterboard, have the following phrases written down:
- Died on the cross
- Created the world
- Had twelve disciples
- Pushes us to work for a better world
- Is present in worship
- Loves us
- Talked to Moses at the Burning Bush
- Gives to each of us a gift
- Born in a manger
- Comforts us when we are sad or lonely

As you read each phrase, have the groups decide which name for God we usually associate with each of this action. If they think that it is the card that they have, have them tape one of their cards next to the phrase. (There may be more than one answer for some of the phrases. The important point is that they begin to see that we think of God in three ways.)

A Dramatic Encounter: The Story of Pentecost

Ask for volunteers to take parts in the following dramatic encounter. Give each player a script and allow them a few moments to familiarize themselves with their part.

Parts:

Reader One

Reader Two

Reader Three

Wind—2 people, non-speaking role

Fire—2 people, non-speaking role

Props:

Fans, plugged in and facing toward the group

Streamers—red, orange and yellow

One: After Jesus had died, he showed himself to his disciples, and said,

Two: "Don't leave Jerusalem!"

Three: "But wait here for what God has promised you."

One: Jesus said, "John baptizes with water, but you will be baptized with the Holy Spirit!"

Two: Jesus also said, "You will receive power with the Holy Spirit, to be my witnesses, to the ends of the earth!"

Three: The disciples probably murmured to themselves,

One: Baptized with the Holy Spirit? What does he mean?

Two: Power from the Holy Spirit? What does he mean?

Three: But they waited. And, then, the day came, the day of Pentecost,

One: And all the disciples were together in one place.

Two: And suddenly from heaven there came the sound like a rush of a violent wind.

Wind: *(At this time the WIND turns on the fans, so that they are blowing on the group.)*

Three: And fire appeared among them, and it looked like tongues of fire.

Fire: *(At this time, the FIRE throws streamers around the group, letting them land on people, furniture, and the floor.)*

One: And all of them were filled with the Holy Spirit!

Two: And they began to speak in other languages.

Three: At the sound, a crowd gathered.

One: They were amazed and astonished,

Two: To hear the different languages.

Three: Some were confused and asked, "What does this mean?"

One: Others sneered and said, "They must be drunk with wine."

Two: Perhaps the disciples murmured to themselves,

Three: "So this is what it is like to be baptized with the Holy Spirit!"

One: "So this is what it is like to be filled with the power of the Holy Spirit!"

Two: The day of Pentecost was a great day for these new Christians

Three: For they received a great gift.

One: And that gift from God,

Two: Promised by Jesus Christ,

Three: Was the Holy Spirit, who would encourage them and empower them as they took the message of the gospel to the ends of the earth!

Wind: *(Turns off the fan.)*

Fire: *(Takes up the streamers.)*

Creative Movement:

Say: "The Apostle's Creed is a statement of what the Christian Church believes. Nearly every Christian tradition holds The Apostle's Creed as one of its central creeds or statements of belief.

"The Apostle's Creed lifts up the mystery of the Trinity—a God who is one God, yet known to us in three persons—Father, Son and Holy Spirit.

Ask for some volunteers to do creative movement as you read the creed. Explain that as you read the Apostle's Creed, you will pause and they will act out, in mime, the words that you are saying. (Pause where there are...(dots) to allow the youth time to decide how to mime.)

I believe in God the Father, maker of heaven and earth...and in Jesus Christ his only son our Lord, who was conceived by the Holy Ghost and born of the Virgin Mary....he suffered under Pontius Pilate...was crucified...dead...and buried...he descended into hell...on the third day, he arose again from the dead...and ascended in heaven to sit at the right hand of God the Father Almighty...from thence he shall come to judge the quick and the dead...I believe in the Holy Ghost...the Holy Catholic Church...the forgiveness of sins...the resurrection of the body...and the life everlasting.

Litany:

Pass out copies of the litany and invite one of the youth to be the leader.

A Litany of God's Nature

One: We believe in God,

All: Who is one, yet three, yet one

One: We believe in God who created the world

All: And created each of us.

One: We believe in Jesus Christ who died for us,

All: That we might live for him

One: We believe in the Holy Spirit,

All: Who comforts us and encourages us.

One: We believe in God,

All: Who is one, yet three, yet one,

One: Who invites our prayers and loves us

All: Beyond our comprehension

One: In Jesus' name

All: Amen.

Small Group Sharing:

Divide youth into groups of three or four. Provide a copy of the Sharing Questions for each group. Ask each group to choose a leader to report back to the group.

Sharing Questions

1. Name the three parts of the Trinity.
2. Which part of the Trinity is the hardest to understand?
3. What are some metaphors that might help one to understand the Trinity?
4. Which part of the Trinity do you feel closest to and why?
5. Why would we call the Trinity one of God's mysteries?

After five minutes, have the small groups join together. Ask the leaders of the small groups to share their answers to questions 3 and 5.

Creative Response:

Provide sheets of drawing paper and pastels. Ask the youth to be creative, and to draw something that helps them to understand God's nature and the Trinity. They can focus on one part of the Trinity or they can think about three in one. It can be realistic or abstract. When the group has finished, invite each youth to share.

Trinity Prayers:

Pass out index cards. Invite youth to write these three sentence starters on their cards, leaving room in between.

> **Thank you, God, creator of the world for...**
>
> **Thank you, Jesus, savior of the world for...**
>
> **Thank you, Holy Spirit, comforter of the world for...**

Then, invite them to take a few moments to complete the sentences.

Group Poem Prayer:

Invite youth to bring their cards with them and to stand in a circle. Place a candle in the center of the circle and ask one of the youth to light it. Turn down the lights.

Ask for volunteers in each category to read their prayers. Begin the prayer by saying, "Thank you, God, creator of the world for..." and then ask anyone who feels comfortable to read what they have written. Do the same for the last two categories. End the Group Poem Prayer by saying Amen.

Closing:

Say, "Today we have marveled at the mystery of the Trinity, how God can be three, yet one. We have been amazed that the nature of God is hard to understand, yet something we can think about and talk about. We don't have to have all the answers about how it fits together. We can try to understand. But in the end, we have to let God be God, and to marvel at the mystery of it all."

End with your group's closing.

Marveling at God's Grace

Session 6

Preparing for the Experience:

Read the book of Ephesians. In this letter to the church at Ephesus, the Apostle Paul presents a summary of his teachings. In chapter two, Paul explores one of the most important of God's mysteries, God's grace. Verse 8, "For by grace you have been saved through faith, and this is not your own doing; it is a gift of God," has played a central role throughout Protestant history. Paul articulates our inability to save ourselves and our complete dependence on God.

Many of us have trouble receiving gifts. It's easier to give them. When we receive a gift, we feel in debt to the giver. Being in debt makes us feel needy, because we have to acknowledge that we can't do it all on our own. A gift warrants gratitude, and sometimes it is hard to be grateful.

The gift of God's grace is also hard to accept. We are in debt to God, acknowledging we can't do it on our own, and we are put into a stance of profound gratitude.

Youth struggle with the questions of identity. They ask, "Who am I?" and "Am I good enough by others' standards?" By helping them to experience and explore God's grace, you are helping them to see themselves as a child of God—accepted and valued!

Gather the following: Large sheet of newsprint or posterboard, markers, copies of Ephesians chapter 2, copies of Sharing Questions, copies of "An Experience of God's Grace," pencils, materials for Grace Collages, copies of the litany, paper and envelopes for Letters to God, copies of the poem prayer, a candle and matches.

Pray for your time together: God of grace and glory, be with this gathering of youth. Help us to marvel at the mystery of Your grace. Help us to understand Your acceptance of us. Help our group to... Be especially with... Amen.

Suggested Schedule:

As Youth Arrive—15 minutes before start of program + 5 minutes

Invitation & Story—5 minutes

Small Group Sharing—10 minutes

Spending Time Alone—10 minutes

Grace Collages—15 minutes

Litany—3 minutes

Letters to God—7 minutes

Poem Prayer and Closing—5 minutes

As Youth Arrive:

Have a large sheet of newsprint or posterboard on a table, with the title, "Things That We Do Wrong." Provide markers. As youth arrive, have them write or draw a picture of things that teenagers do that they are not supposed to do. (For example, smoking, drugs, lying, cheating.) When most of the youth have arrived, look at the poster and have them explain what they have drawn.

Invitation:

Say, "Today we marvel at the mystery of God's Grace. Grace means that God forgives us, even though we do so many things wrong. That God loves us, just because! Not because we deserve the love. We don't earn grace. Grace is a gift. Through Jesus Christ, God forgives our sins and accepts us just as we are. This doesn't mean that we shouldn't try to be the best people that we can be, but it does mean that we don't need to worry about God not loving us and accepting us."

Story:

Gather the group together in a circle and tell the story of the hymn "Amazing Grace."

Amazing Grace

There was once a young man named John Newton. Newton lived in England in the 18th century. When John was 11 years old, he joined his father's ship to begin a life at sea. He worked for several ships, including working for a time on the coast of West Africa, collecting slaves to sell to slave traders. Eventually, Newton became the captain of his own slave-trading ship.

On March 10, 1748, John Newton was on his ship heading back to England from Africa. There was a terrible storm and it appeared that the ship would be shipwrecked. During the storm, Newton had a dramatic conversion, turning to God and giving his life to Jesus Christ.

Although he continued in slave-trading for the next several years, he eventually became convinced that slavery was wrong. He studied to become a minister and worked for the abolition of the slave trade. He died in 1807, the year that slavery was abolished in Great Britain.

John Newton was also a songwriter. He wrote songs that were sung in church which we also call hymns. His most famous hymn is about the grace of God—a grace which Newton described as nothing short of AMAZING!

In his preaching, Newton often used his life as an example of someone who "once was lost" but was found by God and showered with God's grace.

(To read more about John Newton and the stories behind other hymns, see Kenneth W. Osbeck's book, <u>101 Hymn Stories</u>, published by Kregel Publications, 1982.)

As a group, see how many of the words to "Amazing Grace" you can come up with. Write the first verse on a chalkboard or large piece of newsprint. Ask the group to think about Newton's story, as they look at the words of the first verse:

*Amazing Grace! How sweet the sound
That saved a wretch like me.
I once was lost, but now am found,
Was blind, but now I see.*

Small Group Sharing:

Before the experience, make enough copies of Ephesians chapter 2 so that each small group will have one. Write the heading, "Dear Christians in Ephesus" at the top, and "Sincerely, Paul the Apostle" at the bottom. Fold the letter and put it in an envelope. Seal the envelope and write: "To the Christians in Ephesus" on the front. Divide youth into groups of three or four. Give each group an envelope.

Say: "Imagine that you are a church in Ephesus, Greece in the first century, A.D. You are struggling to understand what it means to be a Christian. One day you receive a letter from Paul, who is a teacher and an evangelist. You are very excited to receive a letter from such an important man. As soon as you receive the letter, you gather together to read it. Read this letter out loud, paying particular attention to anything that Paul says about Grace."

When the groups have finished, give them each a copy of the sharing questions. Ask each group to choose a leader to report back to the large group.

Sharing Questions

1. How would you define God's grace?
2. Is it hard to accept being accepted by God? Why or why not?

3. If you were God, would you have a hard time forgiving and accepting some people? Why or why not?

4. In Paul's letter to the Ephesians, he says that we are saved by grace, not by our works. Why would it be tempting to think that we are saved by our works?

5. Why do you think John Newton called his song, "Amazing Grace"?

After five minutes, gather together as a large group, and ask the small group leaders to share the answers to questions 3 and 4.

Spending Time Alone:

Give each participant a copy of "An Experience of God's Grace." Invite them to spend time alone, thinking about God's grace by using these questions and suggestions.

If you have enough space for everyone to find a place out of sight of others, use it. However, if you are confined to one room, just remind the group to be respectful of each person's privacy.

If you have a group of mostly younger youth (ages 12-14), you might need to lead them through the exercise, allowing them time to fill in their thoughts to the questions.

An Experience of God's Grace

1. Say a simple prayer to God, asking God to be with you in this space, in this time. Dear God, be with me, now, right here. Help me to think about You. In Jesus' name, Amen.

2. Think about all of the people who love you, and all of the reasons why you are lovable. Write or draw them in this space:

3. Think about all of the reasons why you are unlovable, and how hard at times it is for people to love you. Write or draw them in this space.

4. Read this sentence from Paul's letter to Ephesians: "For it is by grace you have been saved, through faith—and this not from yourselves, it is the gift of God—not by works, so that no one can boast." Read over the sentence several times. Write down in your own words what you think this sentence means.

5. Reflect on the scripture passage and talk to God, and listen to God:

God, how can You love me even when I am unlovable?

God, what does it mean that You save me by Your grace?

God, how can I accept something that I haven't earned, that I don't deserve?

How can I accept Your acceptance of me, even when I feel unacceptable?

6. Think about the song, "Amazing Grace" and if you feel comfortable, sing or hum it to yourself. As you read the words, open your heart to God and let God's grace pour over you.

7. End with a prayer thanking God for God's gift of grace: God, thank You so much for Your grace that washes over me, and cleanses me. Thank You for forgiving me, for accepting me, for loving me. I pray in Jesus' name, Amen.

Grace Collages:

Before the experience gather the following materials: sheets of white construction paper, glue, different kinds of tape, pieces of colored construction paper, tissue paper, buttons, small pieces of litter, chenille stems (also called pipe cleaners), colored feathers, old magazines, newspapers and anything else that might go into a collage.

Invite youth to make a grace collage by combining various materials in some type of arrangement or structure that expresses God's grace. Assure them that there is no right or wrong way, and tell them to enjoy their creativity by having fun with the activity.

Litany:

Pass out copies of this litany and invite one of the youth to be the leader.

A Litany of God's Grace

One: God, help us to understand and to marvel at

All: The mystery of Your grace

One: How You love us and accept us,

All: Even though we might not deserve it

One: Help us to accept this gift,

All: That You have given to us in Jesus Christ

One: Help us to feel acceptable to You,

All: Even when we do something wrong.

One: Thank You for Your grace, the sweet sound,

All: Of Your amazing grace!

One: In the name of Jesus Christ,

All: Amen.

Letters to God:

Pass out paper, pencils and blank envelopes. Explain to group that they will now have an opportunity to write a letter to God. At the top of the page, have them put the date. Invite them to write down a greeting to God by simply saying "Dear God," or "Hi, God!" Suggest that they take about ten minutes to write whatever they want to God, whatever is on their hearts and minds. If they want, they can tell God what they have learned about grace and how they feel about it.

When they are finished, have them sign their letter, put it in an envelope, seal it, and put their address on the front. Collect the letters and tell them that you will send it to them in exactly one year.

Poem Prayer:

Invite youth to gather in a circle. Place a candle in the circle and ask for a volunteer to light it. Ask for five volunteers to read the poem prayer in turn.

Water pouring over me, I am

Washed, clean and new.

Surrounded by Your grace, I am.

Behold all things are new.

Your grace wraps around me—

I belong to You.

Out of my lostness, I am found,

I find You finding me.

Amen.

Closing:

Say: "Today, we have explored the mystery of God's grace and marveled at how God accepts us, not because of what we do, but as a gift, given through Jesus Christ. As you go through this week, think about God's grace, especially at times when you are feeling sad, lonely, or unloved. Allow God's grace to feel amazing to you." End with your group's closing.

Marveling at God's Possibilities

Session 7

Preparing for the Experience:

Read the Kingdom parables in the gospel of Matthew:

"The Weeds"	Matthew 13:24-30
"A Mustard Seed"	Matthew 13:31-32
"Yeast"	Matthew 13:33
"Hidden Treasure"	Matthew 13:34
"A Pearl"	Matthew 13:45-46
"A Net"	Matthew 13:47-52

Jesus taught about the Kingdom of God by using parables. The Greek word for kingdom is "basilea," which can mean reign or realm of God. What does the reign of God look like? What could it look like? Jesus answered that question not by giving a didactic explanation, but by creating a world, through a story, and inviting his listeners to enter into that world.

The parables of the Kingdom of God give a glimpse of God's possibilities. What is possible for God? What is possible for our world when we live for God and not for ourselves? What is possible for our futures if we belong to God and to God's community?

Open up the world of God's possibilities to the youth in your group by inviting them to enter the world of parables.

Gather the following: Parable Objects (weeds, mustard seeds, yeast, "treasure," a pearl, and a net), posterboard or construction paper for a sign, markers, index cards with the words of scrambled sentence written on them, Bibles, paper, pencils, copies of the Sharing Questions, copies of the litany, clay for clay creations, tools for clay creations (popsicle sticks and orange sticks work well), copies of the poem prayer, a candle and matches.

Pray for your time together: God, be with us in this experience of marveling at the mystery of Your kingdom. Be with each person in our group. Help them to feel closer to You and to learn more about You. Help our group to... Be especially with... In Jesus' name, Amen.

Suggested Schedule:

As Youth Arrive—15 minutes before start of program + 5 minutes

Invitation—5 minutes

Parables—10 minutes

Small Group Sharing—10 minutes

Litany—5 minutes

Clay Response—15 minutes

Poem Prayer and Closing—10 minutes

As Youth Arrive:

Have the following objects on a table: weeds, mustard seeds, yeast, treasure, pearl, and a net. Next to these things, place a sign that says: What do these things have in common? As the youth arrive, greet them and be available to talk with them. Encourage them to look at the objects and to try to answer the question.

Invitation:

Say: "Welcome to our last experience of marveling at God's mysteries. Today we will explore God's possibilities, which is another way of saying the Kingdom of God."

Before the experience, write out the sentence, "Thy kingdom come, on earth as it is in heaven," on 3 x 5 cards, writing one word to a card. Make enough sets of cards so there is one for every set of partners.

Have youth divide into partners. Give each set of partners a set of cards. Tell the youth that this sentence is one that they have probably heard many times in their lives. Ask them to rearrange the words into a sentence. When they are finished, ask them to let you know, and you will check their answer. Ask them to work silently, so that the other groups do not hear them. When all have finished, gather back in the large group.

Say, "Thy kingdom come on earth as it is in heaven, is, as you might know, a line from the Lord's Prayer. Today we are going to talk about the mystery of God's possibilities and especially about the Kingdom of God. The Kingdom of God is known by many names—the reign of God, the realm of God, the Kingdom of Heaven.

"The Kingdom of God is usually referred to as a paradox of faith. A paradox is something that appears to contradict itself or goes against common sense. The paradox of the Kingdom is that Jesus taught that the Kingdom is already here, but also that it is still to come. One way to understanding the Kingdom is that although it already exists, it is not fully established.

Because the Kingdom of God is hard to understand, Jesus used stories and metaphors to teach people about it. We call Jesus' stories parables."

Parables:

Break into small groups of three or four. Give each small group a parable (from the list at the beginning of the session). Have them read the parable and discuss what they think Jesus was trying to teach about the kingdom. Ask them to then come up with a modern version of the parable, using the same object or a different object.

When all the groups are finished, have them share their biblical parable and their modern version with the rest of the group.

Small Group Sharing:

Divide into small groups of three or four. Give each of the groups a card with one of these questions printed on it:

- What would our community look like if it were a community of justice?
- What would our community look like if it were a community of peace?
- What would our community look like if it were a community of love?
- What would our community look like if it were a community of holiness?

Say: "We have been talking about God's kingdom, on earth as it is in heaven, and about God's possibilities. In your group, talk about what it would mean to have a community that was the kind of community printed on the card. Think about things that others could do and things that we could do, as a group, or by ourselves to make it happen. Take about five minutes to think about this together and choose a leader to share your answers with the larger group."

Litany:

When the groups are finished, pass out copies of "A Litany of God's Possibilities," and explain that during the litany, the groups will have an opportunity to share their answers.

A Litany of God

One: Thy Kingdom come, on earth as it is in heaven.

All: Thy Kingdom come, Lord, and may it be a kingdom of justice.

(Share your idea of what this means)

One: Thy kingdom come, on earth as it is in heaven!

All: Thy kingdom come, Lord, and may it be a kingdom of peace!

(Share your idea of what this means)

One: Thy kingdom come, on earth as it is in heaven!

All: Thy kingdom come, Lord, and may it be a kingdom of love!

(Share your idea of what this means)

One: Thy kingdom come, on earth as it is in heaven!

All: Thy kingdom come, Lord, and may it be a kingdom of holiness!

(Share your idea of what this means)

One: Thy kingdom come, Lord

All: On earth as it is in heaven!

One: And may Your possibilities

All: Become our possibilities! Amen.

Clay Response:

Gather around a table and pass out clumps of clay. Invite youth to think about the parables and about God's possibilities and to create something from the clay.

When everyone has finished, have each person share what they have created and share any explanation they would like to give.

Invite the youth to keep their clay creations or to display them in the youth room.

A Poem Prayer:

Gather in a circle and put a candle in the center of the circle. Ask for a volunteer to light the candle. Turn down the lights. Ask for three volunteers to read the poem prayer in turn. Suggest that they read slowly and with feeling.

Possibilities
All things are possible with You,
God
even the
unimaginable
even the kingdom
Jesus talked about.
Your kingdom
Your community
Help us to make
your possibilities
possible.
  Amen.

Closing:

Say, "Over the past seven weeks, we have been marveling at God's mysteries. We have marveled at the mysteries of God's existence, God's love, God's power, God's nature, God's grace and God's possibilities. I hope that throughout this time of marveling, you have thought about things that you hadn't thought about before, and that you have learned something new about the marvelous mystery of how God is present in our lives."

Give youth a few moments to think about what has been most meaningful to them about this exploration into God's mysteries. Ask them to think of one thing that they will remember, or one thing that they enjoyed the most from the past seven weeks. Then, go around the circle and have each person share. (Don't forget to share what has been most meaningful to you!)

End with your group's closing.

Song Resources

Two good songbooks for youth groups are: The Group Songbook (published by Group Publishing, Inc., PO Box 485, Loveland, CO 80538, 1-800-447-1070) and Songs (published by Songs and Creations, Inc., PO Box 7, San Anselmo, CA 94979, 1-800-227-2188). I've listed songs for each week that can be found in either or both of these songbooks. Feel free to use these or your own favorites. The songs for the first week might be songs you would want to repeat each week.

	The Group Songbook	**Songs**
1. Marveling at God's Mysteries		
"Awesome God"	55	1
"Great Is The Lord"	62	
"More Precious Than Silver"	25	8
2. God's Existence		
"He's Everything to Me"		12
"How Majestic Is Your Name"	71	
3. God's Love		
"It Is Amazing"		154
"Love Won't Let You Go"	102	223

	The Group Songbook	**Songs**
4. God's Power		
"I Will Call Upon the Lord"	28	184
"El Shaddai"	82	157
5. God's Nature		
"Holy, Holy"	3	152
"Father, I Adore You"	41	164
6. God's Grace		
"Amazing Grace"	61	10
"Surely The Presence"		25
7. God's Possibilities		
"Seek Ye First"	67	3
"Do Lord"	74	64